SQUAW PEAK

A

*with History, Geology, Trail Maps, and
Photos of the Squaw Peak Area*

BY
JACK SAN FELICE

FIRST EDITION

SQUAW PEAK
A HIKER'S GUIDE
with History, Geology, Trail Maps, and Photos of the Squaw Peak Area

Published by: **MILLSITE CANYON PUBLISHING**
P.O. Box 1118
Higley, Arizona 85236 U.S.A.

Copyright © 1997 by Jack San Felice
First Printing 1997
Cover Photograph of Squaw Peak Mountain by Jack San Felice
Photographs not otherwise credited taken by author
Cover Designed by Lisa Liddy, The Printed Page Co.

Publishers Cataloging-in-Publishing Data
San Felice, Jack
Squaw Peak - A Hiker's Guide / by Jack San Felice
1st. ed.
72p. : maps, photos
Bibliography: p. A1-A2
Includes index.
1. Hiking--Arizona--Squaw Peak Mountain--Guidebooks. 2. Squaw Peak Mountain (Ariz.) Description and Travel--Guidebooks. Squaw Peak Mountain (Ariz.) History.

Library of Congress Catalog Card Number 97-061094
1-890216-05-4 (soft-cover): $6.95

10 9 8 7 6 5 4 3 2 1

DEDICATED TO
MY WIFE WYNNE, WITHOUT WHOSE INSPIRATION
THROUGHOUT THE YEARS I WOULD NOT HAVE BEEN ABLE
TO REALIZE MY DREAMS.

ACKNOWLEDGMENTS vi

INTRODUCTION vii

    Preface vii
    Disclaimer vii
    A Poem to "Squaw Peak" viii
    The Name "Squaw Peak" x
    Author's Note x

THE MOUNTAIN 1

GARNETT BECKMAN 3

VIEW FROM THE TOP 4
    360° Views from the Top of Squaw Peak 5

VIEW FROM THE TOP - MY FIRST SQUAW PEAK HIKE 6

POINTS OF INTEREST - POPULAR TRAILS 7

LIFE IN THE DESERT MOUNTAINS 11
    Know Your Cacti 12
    Desert Wildlife 13

GEOLOGY OF THE MOUNTAIN 14

HISTORY OF THE AREA 15
    Casa Buena 15
    Grand Canal Ruins 16
    The Army and the Indians 16
    Mining and Squaw Peak 18
    Cattle Ranching Near Squaw Peak 20

SQUAW PEAK - A HIKER'S GUIDE
TABLE OF CONTENTS

THE PHOENIX MOUNTAINS PRESERVE **23**
   The Trail Ordinance 23
   The Park Rangers 23
   Preserve Watch 24
   Volunteers 24
   Permits 25
   Reservable Areas 26
   Phone Numbers 26

HIKING THE TRAILS **27**
   Weather 27
   Ethics for Hikers and Riders 28
   Horseback Rider Suggestions 29
   Safety Suggestions for All 29

THE TRAILS **31**

PERL CHARLES MEMORIAL TRAIL (#1A) **32**

QUARTZ RIDGE TRAIL (#8) **34**

CHARLES M. CHRISTIANSEN MEMORIAL TRAIL (#100) . . **36**

MOHAVE TRAIL (#200) **38**

DREAMY DRAW NATURE TRAIL (#220) **40**

SQUAW PEAK SUMMIT TRAIL (#300) **42**
   The Memorial Benches 43

SQUAW PEAK CIRCUMFERENCE TRAIL (#302) **46**

SQUAW PEAK NATURE TRAIL (#304) **48**

HIKERS OF SQUAW PEAK **50**

APPENDIX **A-1**
  Bibliography A-1
  List of Photographs A-3

INDEX **Index-1**

ABOUT THE AUTHOR . . . . **Inside Back Cover**

Trailhead 7.5 min. Topo Map Coordinates . . . . **Back Pages**

SQUAW PEAK
CLIMBING SQUAW PEAK cir. 1914

ACKNOWLEDGMENTS

Arizona Highways
Arizona Historical Foundation
Hayden Library, Arizona State University
Garnett Beckman
Jack Carlson
City of Phoenix Parks, Recreation, & Library Department
Helen Corbin
Greg Davis
Tom Kuhn
Cyndi Nelson
Ken Nelson
Kathy Reichardt
Tony San Felice
Wynne San Felice
Squaw Peak Hiking Club
Squaw Peak Park Rangers
Elizabeth Stewart
Special thanks to John Nemerovski

PREFACE

Squaw Peak - A Hiker's Guide is a book offering the hiker, trail biker, horseback rider, and history buff, as well as visitors and natives, an informative trail guide along with history, geology, a description of life in the desert mountains, maps, trail photos, weather and safety information, and other useful information on the Squaw Peak area.

DISCLAIMER

Hiking, climbing, horseback riding, and trail biking are all outdoor activities that can be dangerous. The information provided in this book is intended to inform and entertain. The final decision to perform these outdoor activities is always the responsibility of the reader of this book.

It is the reader's responsibility to obtain the necessary skills to read and interpret maps and trail guides and to learn skills in hiking, climbing, horseback riding, trailbike riding, and other outdoor activities. Although every effort has been made to check the accuracy of the trail information, changes do occur due to erosion, flash floods, and manmade trail changes and improvements. You must decide whether the trail and weather conditions are safe and satisfactory for you to initiate or continue your activity. You must judge whether you possess the skills, abilities, and fitness required for your activity.

The author and those associated with this publication assume no responsibility, directly or indirectly, for any damage, injury, or loss that may occur from any of the activities described in this book. This is a guidebook only. Your decisions are your responsibility.

"SQUAW PEAK"

Crunch of stones under foot
in darkness I come to a stop.
Warm breath kisses cool morning air
a staccato ticking out
seconds in the darkness.
I move forward and nearly stumble
and fall
a worn boots lace undone
the culprit.

Bending knees I stoop to the ground
fingers fumbling in the dark.
My breath the only sound
that competes with the far off
cry of a hawk
and carries me to the smell of sage
and earth.

Warmth caresses my face
feathery touch and tingle.
Turning I see a break in the clouds
which unfold
revealing
purple and peach and gold

and red are the fringes
of a cloak
which unwraps itself from the
towering rocks I behold.

The world once again makes itself known.

A path winds past saguaro and brush
and climbs upward slow
no rush
to reach skyward to the peak
named for a gentle woman
of a native people.

I am honored and feel one with
what surrounds me, and embrace
this wonderful opportunity
to reach skyward
and walk the path
and know what quietly surrounds
me.

The world once again makes itself known.

- Tony Felice

THE NAME "SQUAW PEAK"

As the author was writing this book, a controversy arose in America and in the State of Arizona regarding use of the name "Squaw". The author in no way means any disrespect or bias to any ethnic group or Native American group. The author is merely stating the facts and historical nature of the name of the mountain and the trails associated with it.

The author has the utmost respect for the feelings and customs of the Native Americans and others who find this name inappropriate. Squaw Peak is and has been, however, the name of the mountain for more than a hundred years. If and when the name is changed, the author will reflect the change in future editions. According to some sources (unconfirmed as of this writing) the original name was Iron Mountain. The author was unable to confirm this information from any reliable historical source.

AUTHOR'S NOTE

On rocky ridges and trails once occupied by ancient Indians, the young and elderly come to scale the heights where only eagles dared to soar. A lizard scurries by and a ground squirrel darts up a nearby cliff amidst the towering Saguaro, blooming Brittle Bush, and thorny Cholla cacti. High above a buzzard circles looking for food below. This may seem like a description of a far away wilderness area, but it is Squaw Peak Mountain, surrounded now by busy highways and active cities. Squaw Peak Recreation Area is actually part of the Phoenix Mountains Preserve, where on any given day 1000 hikers of all ages may gather to ascend the Summit Trail, the most widely used trail of the Preserve. The close proximity of Squaw Peak to the cities of Phoenix, Scottsdale, Paradise Valley, Glendale, and Peoria, to name a few, make this mountain park a unique experience for all who hike or ride its trails. The park is also a favorite hiking and picnic area of families, friends, school children, and many other groups. Follow me as the history and splendor of Squaw Peak unfolds.

Squaw Peak's name was officially confirmed by a Dr. O. A. Turney in 1910 according to <u>Arizona Place Names</u> by Will C. Barnes, 1935. <u>Arizona's Names</u> by Byrd H. Granger, 1983, states of Squaw Peak "The U.S. Geographical Survey named it Squaw because it seemed hardly large enough for a full-sized buck mountain." There is an old Indian legend, however, that in the early days an Indian buck, tiring of his squaw, would take her to the top of the peak and push her off a ledge. As you sit on this peak, you can see places where such a push would be fatal.

<u>Sheriff Magazine</u> (of Arizona), October 1958, makes this statement about Squaw Peak. "At one time 'salty' cowboys and prospectors called the sharp-topped peak 'Squaw Tit Mountain'." But the latter day pioneer settlers of the Salt River Valley never accepted that name and called it Phoenix Peak, then Squaw Peak. Such names were never acceptable to a better class of settlers who came to the southwest.

Originally the Squaw Peak area was used for grazing and mining.

If you look closely at the peak of the mountain and use your imagination, you can see the face of an "old woman" at the very top of the peak from either Squaw Peak Parkway or Lincoln Drive.

THE OLD WOMAN

The height of the peak is 2,608 feet above sea level. Squaw Peak is the highest point in the Phoenix Mountains Preserve. It should be noted that Camelback Mountain is the highest peak in the Phoenix Mountains, but Camelback is not in the Phoenix Mountains Preserve. The radius of the Phoenix Mountains Preserve to downtown Phoenix is designated **convenient** for day trips and day hiking. Many of the trails were developed for horse usage and are still in use.

Squaw Peak did not become a City of Phoenix possession until 1959 when the area was annexed and a long-term agreement was signed with the State. It later became one of the major rallying points for mountain preservation efforts.

In January 1991 major improvements began on the Summit Trail under a bond issue approved by Phoenix voters in 1988. The trail from the trailhead to the quarter mile mark was rebuilt and reinforced. The Phoenix City work crew built native rock retaining walls and added waterbars and curbs to halt erosion. This work was completed in 1991.

The entire Summit Trail was once decorated with luminaries each Christmas season, but the crowds got so large the Park Service discontinued this practice. The regular hikers miss this beautiful experience.

SQUAW PEAK NEAR LINCOLN DRIVE - 1970

Garnett Beckman of Phoenix, a 90-year-old hiker, is a regular on Squaw Peak's Summit Trail. She has seen the number of people who hike it greatly increase since she started hiking the trail in the 1960's. Garnett has seen the Summit Trail change from a narrow, moderately used trail to a highly traveled climb to the top.

About 1000 people now use the Summit Trail daily. Garnett tries to climb every day and can be seen in her visor and dark glasses in the early morning hours. She knows all the regulars on the mountain, including Tom, Noah, Muffin, Vivian, and Don. The fourth bench up Summit Trail was erected in her honor by her children. The plaque on the bench reads "For Garnett from La and Curt."

GARNETT BECKMAN

Garnett is no stranger to adversity and perseverance. On December 7th, 1941, she was at Pearl Harbor when the Japanese bombed it. She says she was taken off the island by a minesweeper. Garnett is an inspiration to all people who strive to seek the summit. Garnett is a very lively person and loves to tell stories about hiking and her early years on the trails before Arizona was such a "retirement and snowbird Mecca." Garnett likes to have a "picnic" after hiking, which usually consists of fruit and something she has baked, such as her favorite sweetbreads.

Garnett has hiked the Grand Canyon's South Rim Trail the last 14 years and has also hiked in Juneau, Alaska and in the Andes Mountains in Equador. The Govenor's Office honored Garnett in 1993 as one of five seniors at the conference "Mastering the Art of Aging - Thriving in Later Years." Way to go, Garnett!

Squaw Peak, with its easily identifiable, craggy peak, is one of Phoenix's best known landmarks. It also contains the Valley of the Sun's most popular hiking trail among its trails. The view from the top is the big feature. Hikers enjoy a spectacular 360-degree panoramic view of the Valley of the Sun. To the south is Phoenix with its downtown skyline, and beyond it are the South Mountains. The Santan Mountains are to the southeast. To the east close-in is Scottsdale. Tempe is to the southeast. Far out to the east are the Superstition Mountains. Black Mountain, near Cave Creek, is to the far north. The McDowell Mountains are to the northeast. Close-in north-northeast is Paradise Valley. North is Shadow Mountain and Lookout Mountain. Northwest is North Mountain and Shaw Butte and the cities of Glendale and Peoria. To the far northwest are the Bradshaw Mountains. To the west are the White Tank Mountains, and to the south-southwest are the Estrella Mountains.

VIEW FROM THE TOP

When you are at the top of the peak, you can easily see Camelback Mountain, Mummy Mountain, Papago Park, Squaw Peak Parkway, and all the nearby mountains and cities listed above. You can also see parts of some of the various trails described below.

<u>360° VIEWS FROM THE TOP OF SQUAW PEAK</u>

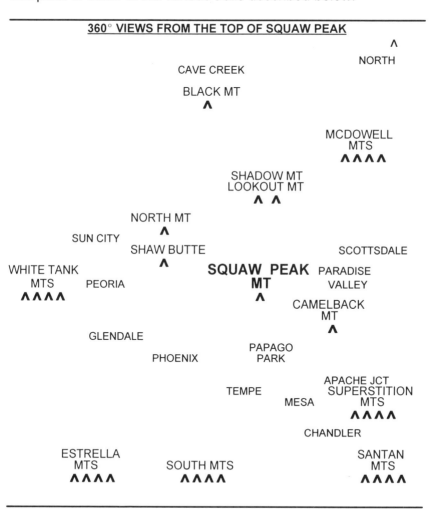

"When I hiked Squaw Peak for the first time, it looked like it was going to be a piece of cake. I saw so many people on the trail as I started up. They were in their 20's, 30's, 40's, and 50's. I saw young children with their parents. There were people jogging up and down the trail as though they were in training for an even harder hike such as the Grand Canyon. I even saw a young man who was physically disabled, and on crutches, attempting to hike as far and as long as he could push his limitations, which seemed endless. I passed a woman who was at least in her late 70's or 80's. I thought, if these people can do it, so can I. It was a wonderful experience. The climb was tougher than I expected. However, it was far from impossible. I took my time and stopped to rest and drank plenty of water, as it turned out to be a very warm day. Taking these much needed rests at the benches on the trail also afforded me the opportunity to see the wonderful views and the rugged mountain scenery that I might

COMING DOWN FROM THE TOP

have not been able to enjoy otherwise. I have somewhat of a fear of heights, so when I was about 35 feet from the top I almost chickened out. If it were not for encouragement from my husband, I probably would have quit then. I am grateful that he did encourage me to continue, as the views of the valley from the top of Squaw Peak are breathtaking."

- Wynne San Felice

- 6 -

The Squaw Peak Summit Trail (Trail #300) is located off Lincoln Drive at the end of Squaw Peak Drive. A two-hour round trip for most hikers, this trail is a **very strenuous** hike to the summit. It is 1.2 miles long and has a 1200 foot elevation gain. The Summit of Squaw Peak is 2,608 feet above sea level.

START OF THE SUMMIT TRAIL

THE SUMMIT TRAIL

Another popular hike is the Circumference Trail (Trail #302) which begins in the same parking area at the end of Squaw Peak Drive.

Follow the trail as it loops around in a northerly direction and winds its way around the base of Squaw Peak. This is rated a **moderate** hike and is listed as 3.74 miles long.

LOOKING DOWN AT THE NATURE TRAIL
WITH CAMELBACK MT IN BACKGROUND

The Squaw Peak Nature Trail (Trail #304) is also located at the end of Squaw Peak Drive and is 1.52 miles long. It is rated a **moderate** hike.

A paved parking area, restrooms, and drinking water are all available at the trailheads for the above trails at the end of Squaw Peak Drive. (NOTE: No dogs are allowed on the Summit Trail.)

Another nature trail near Squaw Peak is the Dreamy Draw Nature Trail (Trail #220) which can be accessed from the Dreamy Draw Recreation Area off Northern Avenue and Squaw Peak Parkway. A tunnel under the Squaw Peak Parkway (State Route 51) is available. This trail has a length of 1.5 miles and is rated a **moderate** hike. A Children's Nature Loop (Trail #220A) is also available. This is a short version of Trail #220. It is 1.25 miles round-trip and is also accessed at the Dreamy Draw Recreation Area.

Parking, restrooms, drinking water, horse troughs, hitching rails, and horse trailer parking are all available at the Dreamy Draw trailhead.

The Perl Charles Memorial Trail (Trail #1A) starts at Dreamy Draw Road and East Loma behind the Pointe Resort. A hitching rail for horses is available at Dreamy Draw Road and Frier Drive. The trail goes east, turns north, and passes through a long tunnel under Squaw Peak Parkway. Here both horses and hikers can enter the trail. Parking is very limited and restrooms and water are unavailable.

PERL CHARLES TRAIL AND SQUAW PEAK

The plaque on the Perl Charles Trail Monument has the inscription "Dedicated to one who has worked endlessly for the preservation of the mountains he loved." It was erected on April 10, 1982. This trail is rated **moderate** to **difficult** and is 4.8 miles long.

The Quartz Ridge Trail (Trail #8) can be accessed from the end of Squaw Peak Drive on the Nature Trail (Trail #304). It descends the valley and then goes between two major washes, passes a large quartz outcrop, and joins the Christiansen Trail (Trail #100). The trail is rated **easy** to **moderate** and is 2.45 miles long.

The Mohave Trail (Trail #200) starts at the Squaw Peak Drive trailhead. This is a multiple use trail suitable for hiking, horseback riding, and biking. It is short 0.3 miles and is rated **easy**. The trail offers excellent views of the city of Phoenix.

The Charles M. Christiansen Memorial Trail (Trail #100) starts at the trailhead at 7th Street and Cherl Drive at Mountain View Park. The dedication plaque at this trailhead reads "The Charles M. Christiansen Trail. A man whose vision and leadership helped establish the Phoenix Mountains Preserve System. Dedicated March 29, 1986." The total length of this trail is 10.7 miles. The trail is rated **easy** to **moderate**.

CHARLES M. CHRISTIANSEN MEMORIAL TRAIL AND SQUAW PEAK

Another trailhead for the Christiansen Trail is located in the Dreamy Draw Recreation Area. The Dreamy Draw trailhead has unpaved parking for horse trailers, a hitching rail, a horse trough, paved parking for cars, drinking water, and restrooms.

The Sonoran Desert has beautiful plant life and interesting animal life. Flora of the desert mountains include almost all varieties of Arizona cacti including Saguaro, Barrel, Hedgehog, Pin-Cushion, Jumping Cholla, Prickly Pear, and Ocotillo. Trees and colorful shrubbery include the Palo Verde, Mesquite, and Ironwood trees; Brittle Bush, Desert Lavender, and Giant Sage shrubs; and Desert Agave, Yuccas, Creosote, Fairy Duster, Jojaba, Desert Broom, Chuparosa, and Desert Hackberry.

PHOENIX SKYLINE SEEN THROUGH DESERT CACTI

There are many books on desert flora. A trip to the Desert Botanical Garden is very worthwhile, as is their bookstore.

KNOW YOUR CACTI

For newcomers to Arizona, the **Saguaro** is pronounced *sah-WAH-ro* and is the largest native cactus in Arizona. It can grow to 50-60 feet and can weigh 5 tons or more when full grown. Its white, waxen flower is the state flower of Arizona and blooms April-June. The needles of the Saguaro are straight.

The **Cholla**, pronounced *CHOl-yuh*, and in particular the Jumping Cholla are whitish-green in color and have clusters of small cucumber-like branches that are **extremely sharp and dangerous** and break off very easily. The Jumping Cholla grow 4-5 feet tall. There are other types of Cholla such as the Buckhorn Cholla which looks similar to a buckhorn of a deer when dead and the Chain-Fruit Cholla which grows like a small tree.

The **Barrel** is a short, stubby cactus that grows as high as 6 feet. It has long needles that are hooked or barbed at the end like fish hooks. In April Barrel cacti display yellow or orange flowers.

JUMPING CHOLLA - A DANGEROUS CACTUS

The **Hedgehog** cactus has very sharp straight needles and flowers in April-May with red to bright red/purple flowers.

The **Prickly Pear** cactus has flat pancake-like spiny pads that are eaten by many of the desert animals. It has yellow to red flowers that bloom in the spring. Its fig-like fruit is made into jelly, candy, and syrup.

The **Pin-Cushion** cactus is one of the smallest cacti, usually growing to less than one-foot tall and looking like a pin cushion.

The **Ocotillo**, pronounced *oh-koh-TEE-yo*, has many whip-like stems or branches and grows about 10-15 feet tall. It has orange-like blossoms during April and can bloom twice a year if Arizona has a wet year. Its blooms and buds are edible.

OCOTILLO CACTUS

DESERT WILDLIFE

Among the many kinds of wildlife that thrive in the desert mountains are lizards, scorpions, rattlesnakes, horned lizards and Chuckwalla. The mammal population includes Coyote, Jackrabbit, Cottontail, Havalina, and Ground Squirrel.

The bird population includes Turkey Vulture, Roadrunner, Cardinal, Mockingbird, and Bluebird as well as several species of hawks and owls.

SQUAW PEAK - A HIKER'S GUIDE
GEOLOGY OF THE MOUNTAIN

While the actual rocks of Squaw Peak are very old, the mountain shapes are quite young. They were formed about 14 million years ago as the crust of the earth was gradually stretched from northeast to southwest, elevating mountain ranges and dropping the basins between them. Erosion has been going on much faster. What we see today are the tops of mountains poking up out of a "sea" of their own debris. The type of rocks and mountains in the Squaw Peak area are generally associated with the Precambrian era more than 1700 million years ago. There is also some indication of Paleozoic and Mesozoic rocks in this area.

ROCK FORMATION ON THE SUMMIT TRAIL

The most common rock found in the Squaw Peak area is a metamorphic granite often called "schist." Metamorphic rocks are formed from older rocks that have been subjected to great heat and pressure or chemical changes. Schist is defined as a metamorphic type of rock with a parallel orientation of abundant mica flakes such that it breaks easily along parallel planes. Rock colors vary between silver-white, gray, yellow, and brown. Minerals of many kinds are found in schist.

CASA BUENA

Not far from Squaw Peak is the Casa Buena ruins of the Hohokam Indians, the ancient Indians who built the canals and farmed the Salt River Valley from 700 A.D. to about 1450 A.D.

Casa Buena was discovered by the Hemenway Southwest Expedition of 1887-1889 and named by Omar A. Turney in 1929. Turney was the City of Phoenix Engineer at the time. Casa Buena was first excavated just east of 20th Street near Yale and Sheridan Streets. Located were Hohokam pithouses, work areas, burial areas, pots, pot shards, and other artifacts such as marine and freshwater shells, stone tools like manos and metates, and animal bones. Casa Buena was a highly organized village from 1100-1450 A.D. Most of the Hohokam sites, including Casa Buena, were abandoned about 1450 A.D. Archeologists are not sure why the Hohokams disappeared. Some think the trade routes collapsed. Others think the Hohokam had to leave because they could not produce enough food to feed their people.

The old Pima stories say the ruins were left by people who had been reduced in number by plagues. The real reason for the end of the Hohokam culture is still a mystery. Many feel that the Pima and Tohono O'Odham (Papago) are their modern descendants. Pueblo Grande Museum is now the repository for the Casa Buena artifacts.

GRAND CANAL RUINS

The Grand Canal Ruins were located and identified by Frank Midvale and are located near the Squaw Peak Parkway. The Salt River Valley contains about 250 miles of prehistoric canals, a major accomplishment when one considers they were dug with stone axes and fire-hardened digging sticks. The canals were constructed to form huge branching systems from water supplied by the Salt River. Fragments of the canals located at Casa Buena were 6 feet wide.

THE ARMY AND THE INDIANS

The Salt River Valley lay unclaimed for nearly 500 years. The 1860's, however, began 25 years of turbulence in Arizona. The discovery of gold and silver brought a rush of prospectors and settlers into what had previously been Indian lands. Open warfare began in 1861. Yavapai and Tonto Apaches living in the central mountains saw their lands invaded by prospectors and settlers. No one's life was safe outside the large towns. Travelling was generally after sunset and before sunrise, even on main roads. The history of Arizona is full of stories, much of it written in blood, between the white man and the Indian.

GENERAL CROOK WITH INDIAN SCOUT

To establish the peace, the Army was sent west. In 1865 Fort McDowell was established on the Verde River seven miles above the Salt River. It was the closest post to Phoenix at the time. This location was selected because of its strategic importance for scouting and punitive expeditions against the Yavapai and Tonto Apache Indians.

The Yavapai and Tonto Apaches were nomadic natives who raided Pima and Maricopa Indians and whites alike and then retreated to the sanctuary of the Superstition, Sierra Ancha, Mazatzal, and Salt River mountain ranges.

Five companies of the California Volunteers were established at Fort McDowell in 1865. The fort provided such services as mail, marriage, and constable to the early settlers before such services were available in Phoenix.

The army had many skirmishes and battles in the Arizona Territory. One of these skirmishes took place on September 30, 1872, near Squaw Peak involving Detachment A, 1st Cavalry.

During the Indian Wars Squaw Peak was used as a heliograph post. Messages were flashed from the peak by means of a mirror, using Morse Code, from mountain to mountain to keep the army apprised of Indian movements and to pass on other military messages. The report of the Chief Signal Officer, Assistant Adjutant General Major William J. Volkman, lists Squaw Peak as a heliograph station.

During the Geronimo wars of the 1880's, Sgt. A. J. Robinson of the 9th Infantry was listed as the officer in charge of the Squaw Peak station. The Indians were finally defeated by General Crook and General Miles with the final surrender of Geronimo in 1886. In 1890 the troops were withdrawn from Squaw Peak and the Bureau of Indian Offices took over.

MINING AND SQUAW PEAK

Although there are no recorded gold mines located on Squaw Peak, many old prospect holes and pits indicate past mining activity.

PROSPECT HOLE ALONG THE NATURE TRAIL

Mercury (Cinnabar) mines were worked in the early 1900's in the Dreamy Draw Park area. You can still see some of these old workings along the Charles M. Christiansen Trail if you look closely. These mercury mines are said to be responsible for the name "Dreamy Draw" because of the mental effects of Cinnabar on the miners.

A news article of April 16, 1927, in the <u>Arizona Gazette</u> titled "New Mine Located on Squaw Peak" describes "The opening of a mine, the ore of which runs a high percentage of cobalt, a rare and valuable mineral seldom found in the U.S., on Squaw Peak, within 12 miles of Phoenix, which is believed by mining authorities may shortly develop into a second inspiration, was announced today by Senator T. S. Kimball, well known mining expert. The mine's discoverer, O. D. Merrill is well known throughout Arizona, having mined and prospected here for the last 50 years. He is the locator of several of the most valuable mines in Arizona including the famous Mammoth and Bulldog mines of the Superstition Mountains and the Cinnabar mines close to Phoenix".

(Note: The Mammoth and Bulldog mines were located in the 1890's below the Goldfield Mountains. They are directly across from the Superstition Mountains, alongside the Apache Trail (Route 88) outside Apache Junction, Arizona.)

As you walk along the trails, you can see some of the old mines and dig holes (prospects). Look for quartz or gray tailings, mine waste materials, but don't go too close and stay on the trails.

ABANDONED MINE OFF THE PERL CHARLES TRAIL

Plenty of quartz material is scattered throughout the Squaw Peak trails. The early miners usually looked for these quartz outcroppings as a sign of possible minerals in the area. Squaw Peak area quartz is white with a mixture of red, brown, and/or black. Along the Perl Charles Trail and the Squaw Peak Nature Trail, just off the Squaw Peak Drive trailheads, you can see old prospect holes, tailings, and white quartz outcroppings. Many hikers have walked past these old prospect holes and miners' dreams without knowing what they were looking at.

(Note: Quartz is a hard white, glassy mineral which is composed of crystalline silica, SiO_2, and is considered to be one of the most common rock forming minerals.)

CATTLE RANCHING NEAR SQUAW PEAK

The Squaw Peak area was originally used as a cattle ranching area by the early American settlers. The grassy areas and meadows near the base of the mountain provided good grazing areas for the cattle from nearby ranches. The rainfall supported desert vegetation and stock raising but was insufficient for crops. Phoenix was known as a "cow town" in the 1800's. Several thousand head of cattle roamed in and around the Phoenix area. In 1877 the roads leading out of Phoenix were described as "not much more than dusty cattle trails". The early newspapers advertised cattle for sale at the Arizona Livestock Auction on 19th Avenue. In 1935 the cattle industry's "Cattle Log" listed 41 cattle ranches in Maricopa County, with several around the Phoenix area.

CATTLE RANCHING NEAR SQUAW PEAK

It was Arizona's mineral potential and the lust for gold and silver that drew the first settlers to Arizona's wild, untamed lands. These first settlers were mostly miners. They were followed by the military, then the cattle ranchers, then the farmers. A direct result of the need to provide food for the miners was the development of the city of Phoenix. Phoenix started as a hay camp supplying hay to the soldiers at Fort McDowell and the miners in the nearby Bradshaw Mountains.

Phoenix was first known (circa 1865) as Smith's Station, named after its founder John Y. T. Smith, a former soldier and later a settler at Fort McDowell. Smith took the initials "Y. T.", which stood for "Yours Truly", so he would not be confused with any other "John Smith". Phoenix subsequently got its name, ostensibly, from "Count" Darrel Duppa, an Englishman who was supposedly exiled. He suggested the town be named after the mythical bird that lived 500 years, was consumed by fire, and arose from its own ashes. Duppa, after observing the prehistoric Indian ruins and canals, thought the name Phoenix appropriate for a civilization rising out of the ruins of another.

The gold and silver miners that attracted the cattle ranchers also attracted land developers who saw the need for the development of water for the Salt River Valley. One of these early settlers was Jack Swilling, an ex-Indian fighter, adventurer, and Confederate Army officer who, in 1867, persuaded some of the "Arizona money men" to invest in development of the early canal system used long ago by the ancient Indians. He hired several Germanic immigrants to work on the canals. This early construction was called the "Dutch Ditch", because the workers were often referred to as "Dutchmen".

One of the most famous "Lost" goldmines in America, located in the nearby Superstition Mountains, was named after an early worker on the "Dutch Ditch", Jacob Waltz. Waltz was the finder of what has come to be called the "Lost Dutchman Mine". He died without filing a claim or leaving a map to the mine. Just before he died in 1891, however, he told his caretaker Julia Thomas and her young adopted son Rinehardt Petrach how to get to the mine and gave them the gold that was in a box under his bed. They began a search for the mine that has involved thousands of people searching the mountains for "Jakes Gold". The mine has yet to be located, although several people have claimed to have found it over the last 100 plus years. The mine is still "Lost", and people still search for it to this day.

RAY HARLAN, THE "OLD DUTCHMAN", WITH THE SUPERSTITION MOUNTAINS IN THE BACKGROUND

(Note: Several good books are available on the "Lost Dutchman Mine" in local bookstores and the Superstition Mountain Museum in the historic town of Goldfield, Arizona.)

THE TRAIL ORDINANCE

To ensure that our fragile desert environment is protected for future generations, the Phoenix City Council approved the Trail Ordinance on June 30, 1993. It defines designated and non-designated trails based on the protection of natural, cultural, historical, and other resources of the parks and mountains preserve.

THE PARK RANGERS

The Park Rangers program was started in 1971. The Rangers perform many roles from educators to security officers. They patrol the parks by vehicle and on horseback.

PARK RANGERS ON THE CIRCUMFERENCE / NATURE TRAIL

The Rangers also provide a program on desert awareness, guided hikes, outdoor survival workshops, and other special events.

Contact the Rangers office at 262-7901 for more information.

PRESERVE WATCH

The city works hard to keep its desert mountain parks and preserves beautiful. However, some park users do violate the park rules. Help protect the environment by reporting any violations. DO NOT personally confront any violator! Call the Park Ranger Dispatch at 262-PARK or the Phoenix Police at 911.

VOLUNTEERS

Citizens have helped shape the mountains preserve program since its beginning. Some groups help in maintenance and re-vegetation in the preserve and perform litter patrol. Others work with a political focus for funding and security. Individuals who want to volunteer can find a variety of opportunities available. They can work with Park Rangers on clean-up projects, trail maintenance and repair, signage, re-vegetation and educational programs, and/or hikes. To become involved, contact the Volunteer Coordinator at 495-5078.

SIGN AT SQUAW PEAK TRAILHEAD

The Squaw Peak Hiking Club was one of the first groups to volunteer. Since their formation, however, many groups have joined with the City of Phoenix Parks, Recreation, and Library Department to help keep the Preserve safe and clean.

The following information is a list of groups that have provided volunteer work around Squaw Peak Recreation Area. This list is from 1994 to the present. I hope all have been included.

+ Squaw Peak Hiking Club
+ Mountaineers, Inc.
+ Boy Scouts of America
+ National Charity League
+ Mountain Bike Association
   of Arizona
+ Squaw Peak Hikers
+ Valley Forward
+ S A & B Environmental
+ Phoenix Mountains
   Preservation Council
+ Youth Service Day
+ Volunteer Center of
   Maricopa County
+ Arizona Public Service
   Kactus Kickers

+ Point Tapitio Stables
+ Stoney Mountain Boarding
   Stables
+ Blackhawk Stables
+ Arizona Road Racers
+ Greenway High School
+ Girl Scouts of America
+ Dobson High School
   Environmental Club
+ Make-A-Difference
+ Temple Chai
+ Popular Outdoor
+ Beth-EL
+ CHAMPS
+ Brownies
and the ...

Phoenix Parks, Recreation, and Library Department's Ranger Cadets and Watch Volunteers

PERMITS

To ensure the safety and enjoyment of all park users, certain activities require permits. Permits can be obtained at the Northeast District Parks and Recreation Office, 17642 North 40th Street, Phoenix, AZ 85032. Their phone number is 262-6696.

ALCOHOL BEVERAGE PERMIT - Alcohol (beer only) is only allowed in certain areas of the park. Permits can be purchased in person for $3.00 at any Parks and Recreation district office during business hours, Monday through Friday.

- 25 -

MUSIC PERMIT - A permit is required to play amplified music in the park. Permit requests must be made in writing with a confirmed reservation two weeks in advance.

CATERING PERMIT - Permit requests must be made in writing with a confirmed reservation two weeks in advance.

RESERVABLE AREAS

Both reservable and open areas are available for group functions in both the Squaw Peak and the Dreamy Draw Recreation Areas. For reservations call 495-0222.

SQUAW PEAK RECREATION AREA
Reservable Areas

Apache	7 tables, 150 people
Hopi	4 tables, 80 people
Mohave	6 tables, 120 people

Open Areas

Navajo	8 tables, 90 people

DREAMY DRAW RECREATION AREA
Reservable Areas

Area A	4 tables, 50 people
Area B	4 tables, 50 people

Open Areas
11 uncovered areas with grills

PHONE NUMBERS

+ Parks, Recreation, and Library Department - 262-6861
+ Vandalism or Park Trouble (Police and Fire) - 911
+ Park Rangers - 262-PARK
+ Phoenix Mountains Preserve - 262-7901

WEATHER

Summer in the Phoenix area is hot and dry, but winters are warm and pleasant. Ask anyone why he or she came to Arizona, and you will probably find the reason to be the weather. Sunshine is abundant here, and it hardly ever rains. Even in the "cold" season, the sun still shines brightly almost every day.

PHOENIX AVERAGE HIGH / LOW TEMPERATURES BY MONTH

	JAN	FEB	MAR	APR	MAY	JUN	JUL	AUG	SEP	OCT	NOV	DEC
HIGH:	65	69	75	84	93	102	105	102	98	88	75	66
LOW:	38	41	45	52	60	68	78	76	69	57	45	39

The best season for hiking and horseback riding is October through early May. You can, however, hike and ride in the mountains during the summer if you take the proper safety measures.

1.   On hot days go very early in the morning, wear light clothing, and take plenty of water.

2.   Do not climb to the summit. Take shorter than normal hikes and rides.

3.   Wear clothing over arms and legs if you sunburn easily or wear a sun block. Wear a hat.

4.   Rest periodically in the shade.

5.   When hiking in cool weather, wear proper clothing for warmth.

Remember, temperatures can vary from 38 degrees (or less) in January to 105 degrees (or more) in July.

The average rainfall for the Phoenix area is a low average of one day per month in May and June to a high average of five days in August. The Monsoon rains occur usually in July and August and raise the humidity somewhat. The higher humidity combined with the higher temperatures creates a higher *apparent temperature rating*.

NATIONAL WEATHER BUREAU ANNUAL RAINFALL COMPARISON BY CITY

```
CITY              RAINFALL
-----------       --------
PHOENIX              7.1"
BOSTON             42.5"
CHICAGO            34.4"
MIAMI              59.8"
MINNEAPOLIS        25.9"
NEW YORK           40.1"
SEATTLE            38.6"
```

ETHICS FOR HIKERS AND RIDERS

1.   Keep to the Trails. Cross cutting creates erosion and destroys vegetation.

2.   Leave flowers, rocks, and cacti in place.

3.   Do not deface the desert with graffiti. Respect Indian Petroglyphs if you see them.

4.   Pack it in, pack it out. Do not leave non-biodegradable objects (like bottles, wrappers, and cans).

5.   Be very careful if you are a smoker to extinguish all cigarettes and matches.

6.   Avoid creating loud noises with radios.

7.   Respect the safety of others. Do not run past hikers on steep or narrow trails (especially the Summit Trail). When overtaking hikers, allow the slower hiker time to move over.

8.   Bikers and hikers should <u>yield</u> to horseback riders. Act with courtesy on the trail. Horses have the right of way to other trail users. If possible, hikers should step off on the downhill side of the trail.

HORSEBACK RIDER SUGGESTIONS

1.   A canteen of water for the rider is adequate. However, there is little or no water for the horses on the trails.

2.   Someone in the party should have a good first aid kit. Bring a comb, pliers, or tweezers to pick out cactus needles. A cell phone is also a handy item today.

3.   Levi's, jeans, or chaps are necessary due to catclaw, cactus, and brush. Wear a hat with a brim and shoes or boots with a heel to avoid slipping in the stirrups.

SAFETY SUGGESTIONS FOR ALL

1.   Always leave word with someone of your destination, and arrival time back home. Always hike with a buddy if possible.

2.   Groups always have slower and faster hikers. Have an experienced hiker bring up the rear. Take a cell phone if available.

3.   Stay on the trails. You may loosen rocks that will roll down and possibly injure someone below you. Stay away from prospect holes.

4.   **Take plenty of water. This is CRITICAL!**

5.   Watch for weather changes and dress accordingly. Wear a hat, sunscreen, and sunglasses.

6.   Take a first aid kit or at least a comb or tweezers for cactus needles.

7.   Wear good shoes and good socks that fit properly. Bring a change of shoes and socks for after the hike.

8.   Hiking downhill is usually more dangerous than uphill. The muscles become rubbery and falling occurs more often downhill. Take your time, especially if you are not in good hiking shape. Many hikers fall when close to the end of the trail.

9.   Take short hikes first and then gradually take longer ones.

10.   Leave valuables at home. Lock your car and place important items in the trunk. Bring a spare car key.

11.   Park Rangers say most injuries are caused by overheated or exhausted hikers. Follow all safety precautions above and drink plenty of fluids even if you feel you are not thirsty. Rest frequently and **do not overdo it**. Respect your own limitations.

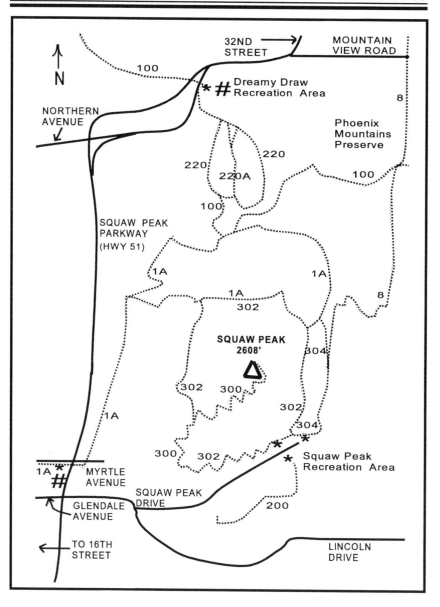

SQUAW PEAK - A HIKER'S GUIDE
PERL CHARLES MEMORIAL TRAIL (#1A)

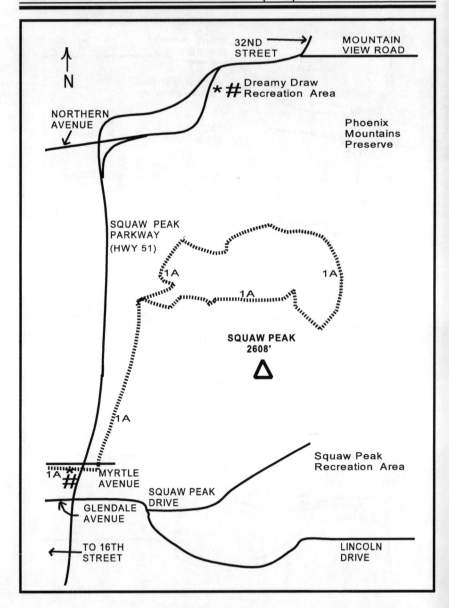

The Perl Charles Memorial Trail is one of the most scenic and challenging trails in the Phoenix Mountains Preserve. This trail is

approximately 4.8 miles long, ascends from a low of 1340' to a high of 2200', and has a difficulty rating of **moderate**. This is a major equestrian trail. It is also popular with hikers and those wanting to study the natural beauty in the

VIEW FROM PERL CHARLES MEMORIAL TRAIL

Phoenix Mountains Preserve. The trail is marked with triangular signs with a "1A" inside a horseshoe logo.

This trail is generally accessed from one of two trailheads (*). The primary access point is at Myrtle Avenue and the Squaw Peak Parkway. There is a horse staging area (#) at this location for equestrians. Alternatively, the trail can be accessed at the intersection of 16th Street and the Arizona Canal (off the map on the facing page) just north of Glendale Avenue and south of Myrtle Avenue. Equestrians can also stage at the Dreamy Draw Recreation Area and pick up this trail where it intersects with the Charles M. Christiansen Memorial Trail (#100) or at Dreamy Draw Road and East Loma behind the Pointe Resort.

Perl Charles was instrumental in establishment of the Phoenix Mountains Preserve and the trails within the Preserve.

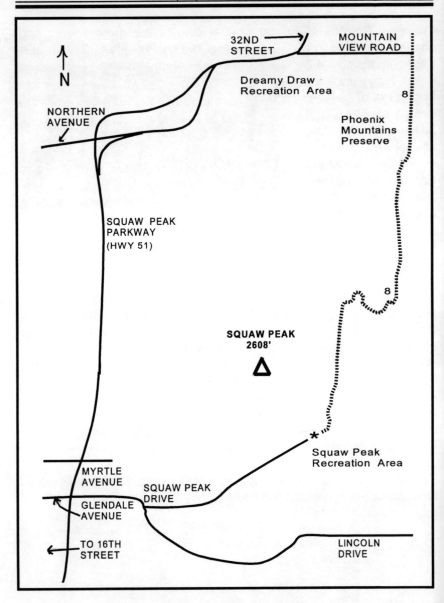

The Quartz Ridge Trail is open to hikers, horseback riders, and bikers. The trail passes through one of the most remote regions within the Phoenix Mountains Preserve. The canyons along this trail feature dense vegetation and are popular with naturalists. The trail is approximately 2.4 miles long, ascends from a low of 1640' to a high of 1860', and has a difficulty rating of **moderate**.

This trail can be accessed from either the northern or southern trailheads (*). The northern trailhead is located at 40th Street and Shea Boulevard (off the top of the map shown on the facing page) and offers unimproved parking for both cars and horse trailers. The southern trailhead is located at the end of Squaw Peak Drive off Lincoln Drive and offers improved parking for cars, drinking water, and restroom facilities.

VIEW FROM THE QUARTZ RIDGE TRAIL

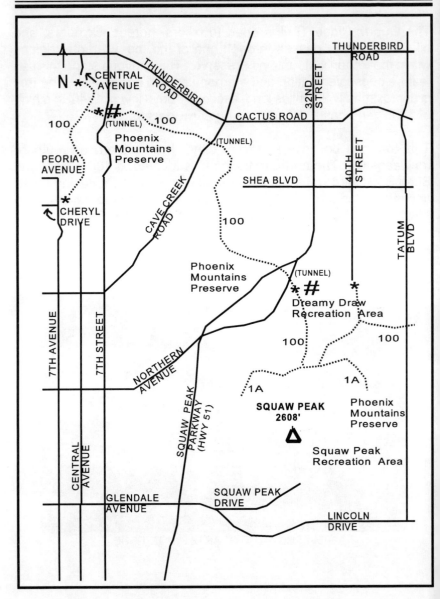

The Charles M. Christiansen Memorial Trail is used for hiking, running, horseback riding, and mountain bicycling. This trail is approximately 11 miles long, ascends from a low of 1290' to a high of 2080', and has a difficulty rating of **moderate**. Actual mileage will vary depending upon the trailhead (*) selected for entry and exit. This trail intersects several other trails in the Squaw Peak Recreation Area which may be taken to vary the length, course, and/or difficulty of the hike. Backpackers often use this trail to prepare for extended hikes.

This trail can be accessed from many different trailheads as seen on the map on the facing page. Primary access to the trail is generally from North Mountain Park off 7th Avenue and Cheryl Drive, the Dreamy Draw Recreation Area, or 40th Street south of Shea Boulevard. Excellent horse staging areas (#) are located at the North Mountain Park and Dreamy Draw trailheads. The trail passes through tunnels under all major streets for the safety of all trail users and horses.

Charles M. Christiansen was a former director of the Phoenix Parks, Recreation, and Library Department. In the 1970's he was instrumental in the establishment and preservation of the Phoenix Mountains Preserve.

VIEW FROM THE CHRISTIANSEN TRAIL TRAILHEAD

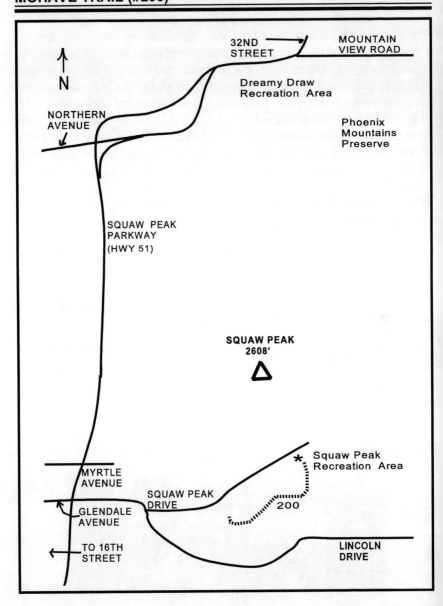

The Squaw Peak Mohave Trail may be used by bikers, hikers, or equestrians. Because of its short length, however, it does not offer the biker or horseback rider the recreational experience offered by other trails within the Phoenix Mountains Preserve. The trail does provide an excellent view of the city of Phoenix.

The Mohave Trail is approximately 0.4 miles long, ascends from a low of 1480' to a high of 1788', and has a difficulty rating of **easy** to **moderate**. The trailhead is located in the park's main parking area off Squaw Peak Drive. Return to the trailhead is accomplished by retracing the trail back to the parking lot.

SQUAW PEAK PARK ENTRANCE NEAR THE MOHAVE TRAIL

SQUAW PEAK - A HIKER'S GUIDE
DREAMY DRAW NATURE TRAIL (#220)

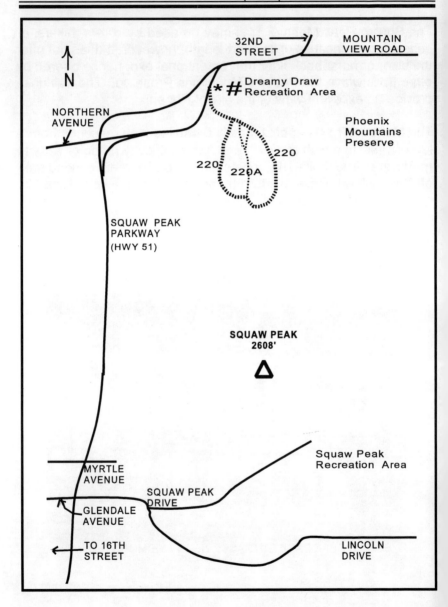

The Dreamy Draw Nature Trail can be used for hiking, running, horseback riding, and mountain bicycling. The trail is primarily intended, however, for those who simply want to enjoy the flora and fauna of the area. This trail is approximately 1.52 miles long and has a difficulty rating of **moderate**. A Children's Nature Loop (#220A) may be followed by those preferring a shorter hike. The children's loop shortens the hike to approximately 1.25 miles.

This trail is accessed from the Dreamy Draw Recreation Area off Northern Avenue and the Squaw Peak Parkway. A tunnel under the parkway is provided for hikers and horses.

The Dreamy Draw Recreation Area trailhead has parking facilities for both cars and horse trailers, restrooms, drinking water, horse troughs, and hitching rails.

VIEW FROM THE DREAMY DRAW AREA

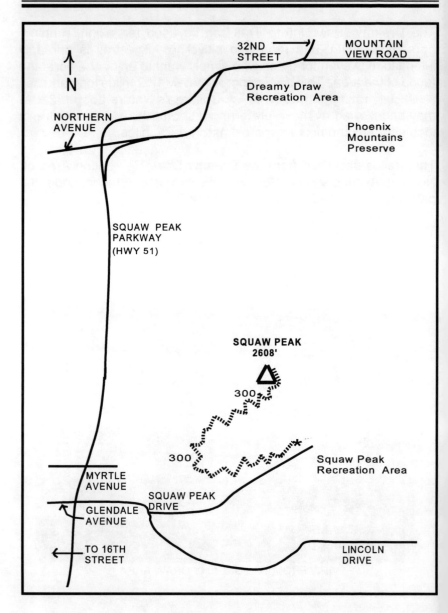

The Squaw Peak Summit Trail is one of the most popular trails in the area for those seeking a good physical fitness workout. The trail is approximately 1.2 miles long and is very steep in places, ascending from 1480' to 2608'. The Summit Trail hike is rated **difficult** and should be attempted only by persons in good physical condition. This hike should generally be taken in the early morning or late afternoon hours, **not** in the middle of the day under the hot Arizona sun. In addition, proper footwear and an adequate supply of drinking water are essential for hikers of this trail. Benches are available at intervals along the trail for those who need to sit for a while and rest.

The Summit Trail and the summit itself offer excellent views of both Phoenix and the surrounding area. In addition, a variety of desert vegetation and animals can be seen along this hike.

The original Summit Trail was built around 1930 by a wrangler working at the Biltmore Hotel. The current trail is accessed from the park's main parking area off Squaw Peak Drive.

The Summit Trail begins in the parking area and ends at the summit of Squaw Peak. Return to the parking area is accomplished by retracing the same trail coming down from the peak.

THE MEMORIAL BENCHES

Five memorial benches (shown on the following two pages) have been erected along the Squaw Peak Summit Trail. These five benches provide a welcome relief to hikers attempting to reach the summit on this difficult trail. The first three benches are also available to hikers of the Squaw Peak Circumference Trail (#302) which separates from the Summit Trail at the third bench.

In memory of
Bruce Allen Smith

- Inscribed -
"In memory of Bruce Allen Smith
1950-1991"

BENCH #1 - BRUCE ALLEN SMITH

In memory of
Robert D. Hill

- Inscribed -
"In memory of Robert D. Hill,
Sooner Born - Sooner Bred,
1927-1979"

BENCH #2 - ROBERT D. HILL

In memory of
Patricia Ann Redivo

- Inscribed -
"In loving memory,
Patricia Ann Redivo,
1943-1992,
Bless - Bless"

BENCH #3 - PATRICIA ANN REDIVO

BENCH #4 - GARNETT BECKMAN

In honor of
Garnett Beckman

- Inscribed -
"For Garnett,
from La and Curt"

In memory of
Kim Lambert

- Inscribed -
"Dedicated to those who
persevere,
In memory of
Kim Lambert,
1955-1980"

BENCH #5 - KIM LAMBERT

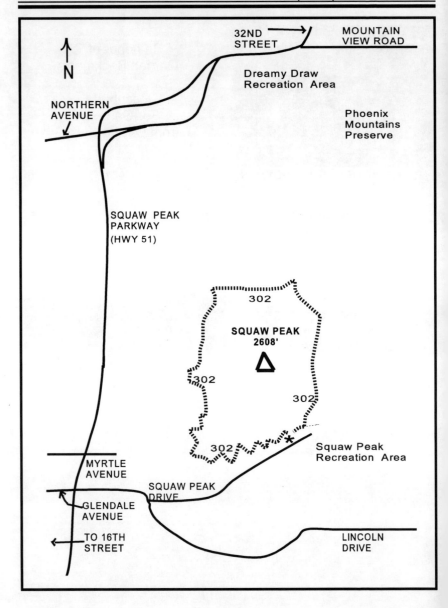

The Squaw Peak Circumference Trail offers an opportunity to explore some of the most scenic areas of the Phoenix Mountains Preserve. A diversity of desert vegetation can be found along this trail. The trail is approximately 3.2 miles long, ascends from a low of 1290' to a high of 2120', and has a difficulty rating of **moderate**.

This trail is accessed from the trailhead (*) at the end of Squaw Peak Drive off Lincoln Drive. This trail coincides with several other trails along most of its route including the Squaw Peak Summit Trail (#300), the Squaw Peak Nature Trail (#304), and the Perl Charles Memorial Trail (#1A). As a result, hikers of the Circumference Trail have several opportunities to vary the course, distance, scenery, and/or difficulty of their hikes.

PHOENIX SKYLINE SEEN FROM THE CIRCUMFERENCE / SUMMIT TRAIL

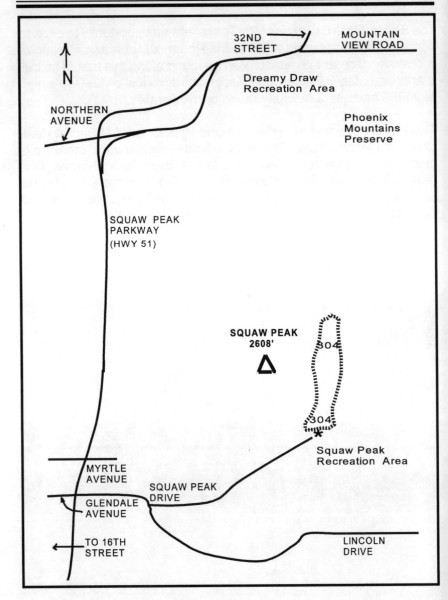

The Squaw Peak Nature Trail is used for hiking, horseback riding, and mountain bicycling. Its primary purpose, however, is to educate the users of the trail on the flora and fauna associated with the area. The <u>Squaw Peak Nature Trail Guide</u> (available through Parks and Recreation offices and Phoenix Public Libraries) is used with the numbered posts along the trail for this purpose.

This trail is approximately 1.5 miles long, ascends from a low of 1610' to a high of 1790', and has a difficulty rating of **moderate**. The trail coincides with the Squaw Peak Circumference Trail (#302), the Quartz Ridge Trail (#8), and the Perl Charles Memorial Trail (#1A) over much of its route.

This trail is accessed from the trailhead (*) at the end of Squaw Peak Drive off Lincoln Drive. Paved parking, drinking water, and restroom facilities are available at the trailhead.

SQUAW PEAK NATURE TRAIL TRAILHEAD

Hikers of the trails in and around the Squaw Peak Recreation Area (including the difficult Squaw Peak Summit Trail) come from all walks of life and all age groups. They include local residents, visitors from other states and other countries, babies in backpacks, small children, and octogenarians. Pictured below is Garnett Beckman (age 90) with family and friends after returning from a hike to the summit along the Summit Trail.

HIKERS OF SQUAW PEAK

Pictured above in the first row (left to right) are Isabel Fierros, Baby Max Beckman (grandson), Chus Tamara (Spanish exchange student), Garnett Beckman, Suzanne Starr, and Curtis Beckman (son). In the second row (left to right) are Sonny Pfund Heller, Baby Jackson Pfund Heller (grandson), Helen Wolf, Kathy Hughes, Jean Sammon, and Dick Wolf.

BIBLIOGRAPHY

Arizona - A Short History; Odie B. Falk; University of Oklahoma Press; Norman, Oklahoma; 1975

Arizona Days and Ways Magazine; February 1960

Arizona Gazette; Phoenix, Arizona; "New Mine Located on Squaw Peak"; April 16, 1927

Arizona Historical Foundation - Hayden Library; Arizona State University; Tempe, Arizona 85287

Arizona's Names; Byrd Howell Granger; Falconer Publisher; Tucson, Arizona 85703; 1983

Arizona Place Names; Will C. Barnes; University of Arizona Press; Tucson, Arizona; 1935

Arizona State Trails Guide; Guide #1; 3rd Edition; Arizona State Parks; 1300 W. Washington Street; Phoenix, Arizona 85007

City of Phoenix Parks, Recreation, and Library Department;1346 E. Mountain Avenue; Phoenix, Arizona 85040

Day Hikes and Trail Rides In and Around Phoenix; Roger and Ethel Freeman; Gem Guide Books; Baldwin Park, California 91706; 1991

General Crook in Indian Country; John C. Bourke; The Filter Press; Palmer Lake, Colorado; 1974

Hiker's Guide to the Superstition Wilderness; Jack Carlson and Elizabeth Stewart; Clear Creek Publishing; Tempe, Arizona; 1995

BIBLIOGRAPHY

Historical Register of the Army - (Chronological List of Battles and Actions of the Army); Frances B. Heitman; Volume 1; Government Printing Office; Washington, DC; 1903

Phoenix Mountains Preserve Brochure; City of Phoenix Parks, Recreation, and Library Department; February 1992

Phoenix Mountains Preserve Designated Trails Guide; City of Phoenix Parks, Recreation, and Library Department; Northeast District

Roadside History of Arizona; Marshall Trimble; Mountain Press Publishing Company; Missoula, Montana; 1986

Roadside Geology of Arizona; Halka Chronic; Mountain Press Publishing Company; Missoula, Montana; 1994

Sheriff Magazine; Volume XII, Number III; October 1958

Squaw Peak Parkway Archeology; City of Phoenix; Pueblo Grande Museum; 1986

LIST OF PHOTOGRAPHS

<u>Squaw Peak</u> - View from south of Lincoln Drive. v

<u>The Old Woman</u> - Close-up view of the top of Squaw 1
Peak from 20th Street.

<u>Squaw Peak As Seen From Lincoln Drive</u>. 2

<u>Garnett Beckman</u> - A 90-year-old hiker of the Summit 3
Trail.

<u>View From The Top</u> - Cyndi Nelson at the top of 4
Squaw Peak, looking to the northeast towards
Scottsdale Air Park and the McDowell Mountains.
The 360° panoramic view of the Valley of the Sun is
spectacular from here.

<u>Coming Down From The Top</u> - Cyndi Nelson on the 6
Summit Trail descending from the top of Squaw
Peak, looking southwest towards Phoenix.

<u>Start Of The Summit Trail</u> - Cyndi Nelson at the 7
Summit Trail trailhead.

<u>The Summit Trail</u> - The Summit Trail winds upward, ... 7
but smooths out in places and offers places to rest.

<u>Looking Down At The Nature Trail With Camelback</u> 8
<u>Mt In Background</u> - Looking east from three-fourths
up the Summit Trail is a great view of Camelback
Mountain, Paradise Valley, the Nature Trail, and the
Circumference Trail.

LIST OF PHOTOGRAPHS

<u>Perl Charles Trail and Squaw Peak</u> - Looking east to. 9
Squaw Peak from the Perl Charles Trail near Dreamy
Draw. The trail winds past several houses and down
and through a tunnel under Squaw Peak Parkway.

<u>Charles M. Christiansen Memorial Trail and Squaw</u>. 10
<u>Peak</u> - A view from the Dreamy Draw area looking
south. Only the tip of Squaw Peak is seen from here.

<u>Phoenix Skyline Seen Through Desert Cacti</u> - A view. 11
through the Ocotillo cactus on the Summit Trail.

<u>Jumping Cholla - A Dangerous Cactus</u> - Touching this. 12
cactus will prove to be a very painful experience.

<u>Ocotillo Cactus</u> - A tall whip-like cactus.   13

<u>Rock Formation on the Summit Trail</u> - One of Squaw. 14
Peak's many unusual rock formations.

<u>General Crook with Indian Scout</u> - Photo courtesy of. 16
the *National Archives*.

<u>Prospect Hole Along the Nature Trail</u> - A sight easily. 18
missed if you don't know what to look for.

<u>Abandoned Mine Off the Perl Charles Trail</u> - Tom. 19
Kuhn points to some old, abandoned diggings.

<u>Cattle Ranching Near Squaw Peak</u> - Photo courtesy. 20
of the *Arizona Historical Foundation* from the *Bert
Fireman* collection.

LIST OF PHOTOGRAPHS

Ray Harlan, the "Old Dutchman", with the Superstition 22
Mountains in the Background.

Park Rangers on the Circumference / Nature Trail - 23
Taking a load of supplies to help rebuild a trail.

Sign at Squaw Peak Trailhead   - Wynne San Felice 24
at the Squaw Peak trailhead sign of the Squaw Peak
Hiking Club, one of many volunteer groups.

View from Perl Charles Memorial Trail - Looking north 33
towards Scottsdale.

View from the Quartz Ridge Trail.   35

View from the Christiansen Trail Trailhead - From 37
40th Street south of Shea.

Squaw Peak Park Entrance Near the Mohave Trail. 39

View from the Dreamy Draw Area - Looking towards 41
Glendale and Squaw Peak Parkway.

Bench #1 - Bruce Allen Smith - A view looking south 44
towards Phoenix from Bench #1 on the Summit Trail.

Bench #2 - Robert D. Hill - A view looking southwest 44
over Bench #2 on the Summit Trail.

Bench #3 - Patricia Ann Redivo - Halfway up the 44
Summit Trail, the Circumference Trail splits off at
Bench #3.

LIST OF PHOTOGRAPHS

<u>Bench #4 - Garnett Beckman</u> - Bench #4 on the 45
Summit Trail offers a welcome rest stop *with shade*
just before the final and *steepest* part of the hike to
the summit begins.

<u>Bench #5 - Kim Lambert</u> - The fifth and last bench on 45
the Summit Trail and the first handrail are signs that
you are almost at the top.

<u>Phoenix Skyline Seen from the Circumference /</u> 47
<u>Summit Trail</u>.

<u>Squaw Peak Nature Trail Trailhead</u>.   49

<u>Hikers of Squaw Peak</u> - Garnett Beckman with family 50
and friends after a hike to the top of Squaw Peak and
back on the Summit Trail.

<u>Picture of the Author - Jack San Felice</u>   . . Inside Back
                                                              Cover

Apache Trail 19
Arizona Highways vi
Arizona Historical Foundation . . . . vi, A-1, A-4, A-6
Arizona Territory 17
Army 16, 17, 21, A-2
Barrel Cactus 11, 12
Beckman, Garnett . . . . vi, 3, 45, 50
Black Mountain 4, 5
Botanical Garden 11
Bourke, John C. A-1
Bradshaw Mountains 4, 21
Camelback Mountain 1, 5, 8
Carlson, Jack . . . . vi, A-1
Casa Buena 15, 16
Cattle Log 20
Cattle Ranching 20, 21
Cave Creek 4, 5
Charles, Perl 33
Charles, Perl Memorial Trail . . . . x, 9, 19, 32, 33, 49
Cherl Drive 10
Children's Nature Loop 8, 41
Cholla Cactus . . . . x, 11, 12
Christiansen, Charles M. 37
Christiansen, Charles M. Memorial Trail . . . 9, 10, 18, 33, 36, 37
Cinnabar 18, 19
Circumference Trail 7, 23, 43, 46, 47, 49, A-3, A-5
City of Phoenix, Parks, Recreation,
        and Library Department . . . . vi, 24, 25, 26, 37, A-1, A-2
Cobalt 18
Corbin, Helen vi
Crook, General George C. 17, A-1
Davis, Greg vi
Dreamy Draw Nature Trail 8, 40, 41
Dreamy Draw Recreation Area . . . 8, 10, 18, 26, 33, 37, 41, A-4

SQUAW PEAK - A HIKER'S GUIDE
INDEX

Dreamy Draw Road 9
Duppa, Darrel 21
Dutch Ditch 21, 22
East Loma Road 9
Estrella Mountains 4, 5
Ethics 28
Frier Drive 7
Fort McDowell 17, 21
Geology 14, A-2
Geronimo 17
Glendale . . . . x, 4, 5
Goldfield Mountains 19
Grand Canal Ruins 16
Granger, Byrd H. 1, A-1
Hayden Library . . . . vi, A-1
Hedgehog Cactus 11, 13
Heliograph 17
Hemenway Expedition 15
Hill, Robert D. 44
Hohokam Indians 15
Horseback Riders . . . . vii, 9, 27, 29, 35, 37, 39, 41, 49
Iron Mountain x
Kimball, T. S. 18
Kuhn, Tom . . . . vi, A-4
Lambert, Kim 45
Lincoln Drive 1, 2, 6, 35, 47, 49, A-3
Lookout Mountain 4, 5
Mammoth Mine 19
Maricopa Indians 17
Mazatzal Mountains 16
McDowell Mountains 4, 5, A-3
Mercury 18
Merrill, O. D. 18
Metamorphic Rocks 14

Miles, General Nelson A. 17
Mining 1, 18
Mohave Trail 9, 38, 39
Mountain View Park 10
Mummy Mountain 5
Nelson, Cyndi . . . . vi, A-3
Nelson, Ken vi
North Mountain 4, 5
Northern Avenue 8, 41
Ocotillo Cactus 11, 13
Paleozoic Era 14
Papago Park 5
Paradise Valley . . . . x, 4, 5, A-3
Park Rangers . . . . vi, 23, 24, 26, 30
Pearl Harbor 3
Peoria . . . . x, 4, 5
Permits 25, 26
Petrach, Rinehardt 22
Phoenix . . . . x, 1, 2, 3, 4, 5, 9, 11, 15, 17,
                                       18, 19, 20, 21, 23, 27, 28,
                                       39, 43, A-1, A-2, A-3, A-5
Phoenix Mountains Preserve . . . . x, 1, 10, 23, 24, 25, 26,
                                       33, 35, 37, 39, 47, A-1
Phoenix Peak 1
Pima Indians 15, 17
Pointe Resort 9
Precambrian Era 14
Preserve Watch 24
Prickly Pear Cactus 13
Pueblo Grande Museum 15, A-2
Quartz 9, 19
Quartz Ridge Trail 9, 34, 35, 49
Rainfall 20, 28
Redivo, Patricia A. 44

Reichardt, Kathy vi
Reservable Areas 26
Robinson, A. J. 17
Safety . . . . vii, 25, 27, 29, 30, 37
Saguaro Cactus . . . . ix, x, 11, 12
Salt River 1, 15, 16, 17, 21
San Felice, Jack . . . . x, inside back cover
San Felice, Tony . . . . vi, ix
San Felice, Wynne . . . . vi, 6, A-5
Santan Mountains 4, 5
Schist Rocks 14
Scottsdale . . . . x, 4, 5
Scottsdale Air Park A-3
Shadow Mountain 4, 5
Shaw Butte 4, 5
Sheridan Street 15
Sheriff Magazine 1, A-2
Sierra Ancha Mountains 17
Smith's Station 21
Smith, Bruce A. 44
Smith, John Y. T. 21
South Mountains 4, 5
Squaw . . . . ix, 1
Squaw Peak . . . . . . viii, ix, x, 1, 2, 4, 5, 6, 7, 8, 9, 10, 14, 15, 17,
                        18, 19, 20, 24, 43, 50, A-1, A-3, A-4, A-5
Squaw Peak Drive 6, 7, 8, 9, 19, 35, 39, 43, 47, 49, A-3
Squaw Peak Hiking Club . . . . vi, 24, 25, A-5
Squaw Peak Nature Trail 8, 9, 18, 19, 23, 47, 48, 49
Squaw Peak Parkway 1, 5, 8, 9, 16, 33, 41, A-2, A-4
Squaw Peak Recreation Area . . . . x, 25, 26, 37, 50
Stewart, Elizabeth . . . . vi, A-1
Summit Trail . . . . x, 2, 3, 7, 8, 14, 29, 42, 43,
                        44, 45, 47, 50, A-3, A-4
Superstition Mountains 4, 5, 17, 19, 22, A-1

SQUAW PEAK - A HIKER'S GUIDE
INDEX

Swilling, Jack 21
Tempe 4, 5
Temperatures 27, 28
Thomas, Julia 22
Tohono O'Odham Indians 15
Tonto Apaches 16, 17
Trail Ordinance 23
Turney, Omar A. 1, 15
U. S. Geographical Survey 1
Verde River 17
Volkman, William J. 17
Volunteers 24, 25, A-5
Waltz, Jacob 22
Weather Information . . . . . vii, 27, 28, 30
White Tank Mountains 4, 5
Wildlife 13
Yale Street 15
Yavapai Apaches 16, 17

Trailhead 7.5 min. Topo Map Coordinates

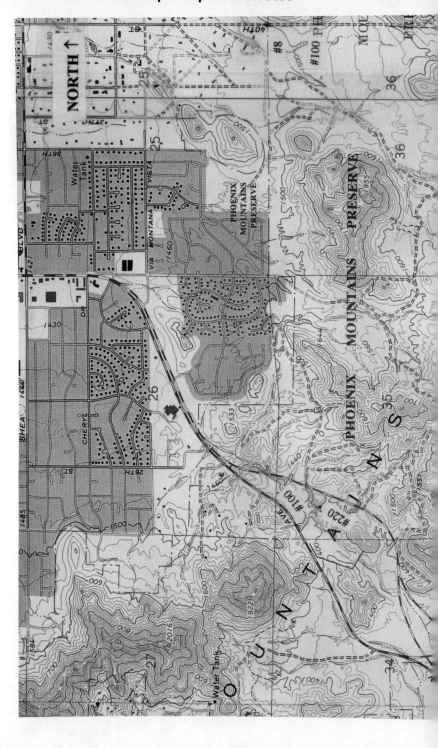

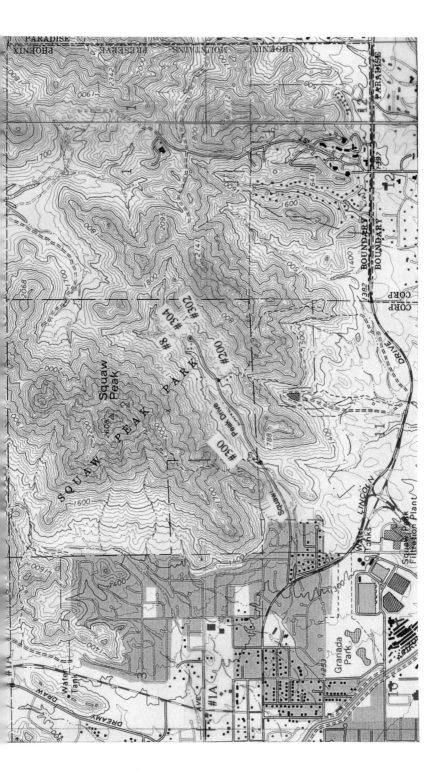

U.S. Geological Survey Topo Map Coordinates
7.5 minute Quadrangle Maps for Sunnyslope & Paradise Valley

Squaw Peak Trail Coordinates

1. Perl Charles Memorial Trail # 1A
Trailhead at Myrtle Ave. & Squaw Peak Pkwy -   N.33° 32' 30"
W. 112° 2' 26"
Trailhead at Dreamy Draw Dr. & E. Loma St.   N. 33° 33' 12"
W. 112° 2' 19"

2. Quartz Ridge Trail # 8
Trailhead at 40th St. south of Shea Blvd   N. 33° 34' 5";
W. 111° 59' 42"
Trailhead at Squaw Peak Dr. N. 33° 32' 33" ;   W. 112° 0' 52"

3. Charles M. Christiansen Trail #100 (North Mt. Park)
Trailhead at 7th Ave. & Cherl Dr. N. 33° 34' 43" ;W. 112° 4' 53"
Trailhead at Dreamy Draw Rec. Area   N. 33° 33' 53"
W. 112° 1' 41"

4. Mohave Trail #200 (Squaw Peak Drive)
Trailhead at Squaw Peak Dr. Rec. Area   N. 33° 32' 28"
W.112° 1' 03"

5. Dreamy Draw Nature Trail # 220
Trailhead at Northern Ave. & Dreamy Draw Rec. Center-
N. 33° 33' 53"
W. 112° 1' 41"

6. Summit Trail # 300 (Squaw Peak Drive)
Trailhead at Squaw Peak Rec. Area -   N. 33° 32' 19"
W. 112° ' 24"

7. Squaw Peak Circumference Trail # 302 (Squaw Peak Dr.)
Trailhead at Squaw Peak Rec. Center -   N. 33°32' 33"
W. 112° 0' 52"

8. Squaw Peak Nature Trail # 304 (Squaw Peak Drive)
Trailhead at Squaw Peak Rec. Area -Coordinates same as #302 above

Jack San Felice has been a hiker and person involved in outdoor activities since he was six years old and his father took him hunting wild game in the hills and mountains of western Pennsylvania. He enjoys many outdoor activities such as hiking, white water rafting, mountain biking, men's softball, rock hounding, off-road 4-wheeling, outdoor photography, and searching for lost mines.

Jack is a native of Beaver Falls, Pennsylvania. He spent 30 years working in the Washington, D.C. metropolitan area after serving in the U.S. Army. He lived in Huntingtown, Maryland prior to moving to the Phoenix area. He attended American University in Washington, D.C. and received his B.S. degree in 1971. He received an M.S. degree from American University in 1974.

Jack served as a police officer with the Washington, D.C. and Prince George's County Maryland police departments from 1963 to 1992 and retired as a Captain. He has written many technical law enforcement and professional documents.

Jack is a member of the Superstition Mountain Historical Society and Guild and is currently a part-time instructor at Scottsdale Community College. He is also a member of the Concepts-To-Operations consulting firm of Annapolis, Maryland and serves as a volunteer photographer for various organizations. He currently resides in Gilbert, Arizona.

NOTES

NOTES

NOTES